New York's Hudson ‖ America's Valley

Hudson Highlands from Boscobel's lawn

New York's Hudson

America's Valley

Photographs and text by

Ted Spiegel

Involvement Media, Inc.
in association with
Friends of the Hudson Valley

Catskill: Coast Guard icebreaker/buoy-tender

This book is dedicated to Amanda, David and Erik

The author offers his thanks to Friends of the Hudson Valley and Jackson Hole Preserve, Inc., for their interest and support.

Library of Congress Catalog Card number 00-107428

Copyright © 2000 Involvement Media, Inc.
Photographs and text © 2000 Ted Spiegel

This book has been produced by CommonPlace Publishing
Editors: Paul DeAngelis, Carolyn Krinsley
Art Director/designer: Samuel N. Antupit
Map: Matthew Bazylewkyj
Guide research: Elizabeth Montgomery
Project Manager for Involvement Media: Aleta Pahl

Involvement Media, Inc.
P.O. Box 1818
Kingston, N.Y. 12401

Printed in Hong Kong
through Global Interprint

Tappan Zee at dawn

The Hudson is a river splendid through four seasons.

Spring begins as shad return home from the Atlantic to spawn in a living river.

Summer winds fill yachtsmen's sails on a sporting river.

Winter's icebreaker cuts channels through a working river.

Fall's colors blaze the valley's welcome to all who come to share in its beauty.

Contents

Kingston: *HMS Rose* at Hudson Maritime Museum

Preface

Step out into the Hudson Valley and you are in a world that reverberates with the voices of the fourth dimension — time. The threads of time spread across these pages represent epochs and eras, seasons and moments. View this book as a voyage. Hear the voices of pre-history: geological time sounding out along winter stream beds, spring peepers and salamanders evoking the emergence of life. See American history come alive with the musket fire of Revolutionary War reenactments and the staccato engine bursts of a World War I flying circus. You never tire of having been there and done that along the Hudson. Each new place visited, each new visit to a favorite spot offers a different experience.

When I was a child wandering through the halls of the American Museum of Natural History on the Upper West Side of Manhattan, no one understood the Big Bang or Continental Drift. Today, the Museum's Rose Planetarium offers its visitors a 13-billion-year voyage through the universe. The geological displays describing planet Earth's 4.6-billion-year existence are awesome. When you leave the galactic space show, do not let yourself be intimidated by the 299-foot circular walk down through cosmic time. Yes, 13 billion years is a long voyage from the unexplainable to now, and when we find human existence represented by the thickness of a hair, who could not feel small? But human curiosity is far broader than a hair. We have become skillful questioners, setting our sights beyond our immediate place in space. Only humans know that the electron field of an atom is 100,000 times larger than its nucleus, that the average distance between Earth and our sun is 150 million kilometers. If you go but a mile west of the Planetarium to the 79th St. Boat Basin on the Hudson and take a boat trip north, you will come eye to eye with 1.3 billion years of geologic time — a full thirty feet on the Planetarium ramp.

This book summarizes the twenty-five years I have spent traveling through the valley. The pages that follow offer invitation, not definition. Informed by geology, biology, history, anthropology or family curiosity, you will find that America's Valley is a great place to enjoy time. Bill Kelly, geologist with the New York State Museum, suggests that "time is what process takes place in." The Hudson offers a lively procession.

Our first chapter delves into the Hudson's geological pre-history and natural setting. The second chapter spans the European pioneer period from Henry Hudson's exploratory voyage in 1609 through Dutch and English colonization, the English colonists' revolt, and the war that established a new nation with its first capital in New York City. Chapter Three chronicles the Hudson Valley as not only gateway to America, but also as seat of culture and commerce. Chapter Four explores through a twentieth century strongly influenced by a President and First Lady from the mid-Hudson; it also offers a foldout map and directory of the valley's prominent sites and sights. From New York City's Broadway, Wall Street and UN Plaza to all of the highways, from 9A to 9W, the Hudson Valley has many addresses worth visiting.

1: An Emerging Land

The river is like a great womb. My job is to get people to look beneath the surface, at the cycle of life taking place underwater.
— Fran Dunwell

Travelers in the Hudson River Valley delight in discovering the viewpoint on Route 6/202, three miles north of Peekskill on the way to the Bear Mountain Bridge. From this perch, carved into the flanks of the stony rampart Dutch Colonists called Anthony's Nose, they look straight down at the Hudson. The well-informed watch the surface closely to see if the river is in flood, flowing north towards its source in the Adirondacks, or at ebb, coursing towards the Atlantic. With two tide changes of four feet daily, and a bi-directional current of three miles per hour, the Hudson River is a true fjord for 155 of its 315 miles. Norway's longest — Sognefjord — reaches only 126 miles into the Scandinavian peninsula. Only as this estuarine arm of the sea reaches the Federal Canal locks and dam at Troy does it give up sea level status. Viewed from this entrance point into the Hudson Highlands, the valley's western shore, with Bear Mountain's 1284-foot summit as its apex, appears in its pristine state.

Anthony's Nose is also a perfect spot from which to view the evolution of the natural landscape. One fourth of earth's geological history can be traced in the rock formations surrounding this viewpoint. Radioisotope-dating has revealed that 1.3 billion years ago Bear Mountain and the surrounding Hudson Highlands began their existence as layers of sand, lime and mud at the bottom of a sea which extended from Labrador to Georgia, and on into Mexico. The earth's magma intruded spurts of molten granite into these layers. As formed continents began to drift towards each other, these lasagna-like layerings of granite, sand, seashells and solidifying mud, thousands of feet thick, were over-run and pushed down twenty miles below where Bear Mountain now stands. Subjected to temperatures of 700° Celsius and atmospheric pressures 6,000 times more powerful than on the earth's surface, the loose sediments were changed chemically and physically — metamorphosed — into granitic gneiss and marble.

Over the next billion years, continents drifted together and pulled apart in four major mountain building epochs. During each epoch, new material was deposited through volcanic eruptions and erosion by scouring glaciers and eroding waters. The pressures exerted by continents drifting atop the earth's molten core stressed, bent, cracked, and uplifted these deposits. During the last major period of continental collision, all of the earth's landmasses were joined together into one super-continent, Pangea.

1   2

Worldwide, the collision fronts created great mountain ranges. A Tibetan-like plateau rose 15,000 feet above sea level at this spot. Rain, snow, and glaciers eroded the lofty range as the super-continent broke into continental plates that drifted east back across earth's molten subsurface to become what is now the eastern shore of the north Atlantic. The 1.2 million-year long Pleistocene ice age, which brought miles-thick glaciers across this region, lasted until just 12,500 years ago. The glacial grindings stacked up a 125-mile long gravelly mound, the terminal moraine we now call Long Island. As the glaciers receded, they revealed the modern Hudson Highlands, then the Catskills, and then the Adirondacks. Today's Bear Mountain is but the basement of the lofty Everest that once towered here.

Iona Island sits amidst the Hudson, just south of Bear Mountain. Researchers who cored to bedrock deep within the flat marshy land on the island's western side have confirmed that as of 12,500 years ago the glaciers had receded from here. As global warming ended the million-year-long winter, glaciers continued to pull back from New York State, and by 8,000 years ago they had drawn back past the St. Lawrence River. Glaciologist Don Cadwell remembers a dawn moment when he looked down from a high eastern hill and "the low dense fog filling the valley's gaps and crevices was like glimpsing the fog created by the last of the receding glaciers. The valley must have looked just like that foggy morning for centuries."

Layer by layer, the valley returned from its million-year-long arctic deep freeze into a temperate climate with four distinct seasons. Organic material built up beneath the water, fish soon found it good habitat, and the surrounding forests, which started out as spruce and fir, evolved first into white pine before eventually becoming today's predominantly oak, hickory and maple stands.

The First Americans settled on the land as the glaciers receded. They thrived here on deer, turkey and such river delicacies as shad, bass, and oysters harvested at low tide. Though war was a necessary means to assure their presence in this "happy hunting grounds," they did not wage war against the valley.

But once the First Owners started selling off their land and control of the river

3

4

A geological chronology from the New York State Museum. *(From left to right:)* 1. A folded stone swan of metamorphosed lime mud more than a billion years old, from Lake George. 2. A cross-section of Rensselaer greywacke formed from pebbles tumbling into the ocean 500 million years ago and "baked" over geologic time into solid rock. 3. A hexagonal basaltic column from the Palisades — a cooled, 200-million-year-old lava flow. 4. A chunk of peat from a swampy depression gouged by glacial ice blocks that melted 18,000 years ago; a handful of gravel deposited on the land surface by the receding glaciers.

to Europeans who "colonized and civilized," the forests came under siege. Old growth cedar stocks were heavily exploited to provide masts and spars for Dutch and English navies. Expanding towns and cities demanded further logging, which created eroding, barren slopes, and eventually inspired America's first natural conservation movement.

By the late nineteenth century, much of the Adirondack region was being bought up by America's newly rich entrepreneurs. This "upper crust" was the first to conserve the land in the Hudson Valley watershed — for their own pleasure. They built personal "great camps," log cabin palaces set amidst 10,000-acre private forests. Before long, the pleasures of the Adirondack and Catskill wildernesses enticed the lesser classes as well. Verplanck Colvin, an Albany man who was the first to discover — and name — the Hudson's highest source, two-acre "Lake Tear of the Clouds" near the summit of Mount Marcy, spearheaded the campaign to create a state park in the Adirondacks. His pleas were rewarded after a twenty-year campaign by a state constitutional amendment guaranteeing that "the lands . . . constituting the Forest Preserve . . . shall be forever kept as wild forest lands."

Hikers like to follow the Hudson's course to Manhattan by first ascending Mt. Marcy, at 5,344 feet the state's highest natural skyscraper, then parallelling the river to the tip of Manhattan Island, home of its man-made skyscraper skyline. The waters of many a summer thunderstorm collect in alpine Adirondack pockets, then cascade across the rocky pre-Cambrian slopes through a lacework of mountain streams. Lake Tear's waters course down the Opalescent River. Within a few miles, brooks fed by Lake Colden and Avalanche Lake join up with the Opalescent as it passes through the Flowed Lands.

Hiking thirty miles down from Mt. Marcy, a traveler can board a whitewater raft at Indian Lake for an exhilarating seventeen-mile, three-hour adventure through a slew of rapids and the grandeur of the Hudson River Gorge. The voyage courses through a wilderness miles from any settlement.

For those who remain on foot, the trails descend into upper Hudson River town parks only briefly. Near Saratoga Springs, gentler angles of descent herald the first sight of the valley. As the mountains of Vermont present themselves, the traveler gains a sense of the great glacial flow that once carved the gap between those distant Vermont ramparts and the evergreen sea of the high peak Adirondacks. The lowlands around Saratoga offer leafy hardwood forests; in autumn the maples stand out in an eye-blazing "hello!"

Canoes can now be boarded to continue a waterborne voyage on a pond-like Hudson. For seventy miles, the river is flattened out by twelve locks: at the beginning of the nineteenth century, engineers of a new nation canalized the Hudson from Troy to Lake Champlain. The much-improved ditch and lock system intrudes on a naturalist's voyage, but waterfowl and fish find this stretch of the Hudson most hospitable.

Once the Hudson's waters are joined by the Mohawk River at Waterford and flow past the Federal Government locks at Troy, the river resumes its natural identity. The waters from Lake Tear of the Clouds now enter the tide-responsive part of the Hudson. From here to New York Bay, cities and towns hug the shoreline, railroad viaducts create backwaters where new marshland has been created, river traffic thrives within a thirty-two-foot channel dredged by the U.S. Army Corps of Engineers and maintained by a Coast Guard Aids to Navigation team based in Saugerties. But the canoeist's selective vision blocks these quickly, delighting instead in the endless vistas of virgin wetlands with their towering grasses and reeds. The over two hundred lights and markers that alert deep-draft vessels to rocky reefs and hidden sandbars are also a welcome guide to the lonesome paddler.

From Saratoga all the way south to the Battery, the backpacker can stay almost without interruption on state and local trails. Thanks in large part to the Hudson River Valley Greenway, a state-sponsored community effort established in 1991, a 150-mile double chain of parks and trails now winds its way on both sides of the river through the more densely populated mid-Hudson Valley to Manhattan. Designation of the Hudson River Valley as a "National Heritage Area" in 1996 brought with it funding to expand and upgrade parklands and improve river access.

Despite the Greenway and similar efforts, conservation has not always been universally accepted by New Yorkers. In the heyday of industrialization, the Hudson functioned largely as a sewer drain, which later environmentalists have been challenged to flush out. One of these is Fran Dunwell, Special Assistant at New York's Department of Environmental Conservation. Dunwell heads the Hudson River Estuary Action Plan adopted in 1996 under Governor George Pataki. This 116-million-dollar program seeks to assure the future of the river by understanding it from the bottom up. "Like your subconscious, it's what's under the surface, what you can't see that really counts," says Dunwell. "Just as your dreams are the voice of the unconscious, the fish are the voice of the river."

For the best description of what's going on under the river surface, we can find no better authority than oceanographer Robin Bell. Dr. Bell operates out of Columbia University's Lamont-Doherty Laboratory on a DEC-funded project that uses ultra-sophisticated side-scanning sonar to map every inch of the river's bottom. The project's primary mission is to look at "benthic habitats" — the river bottoms where fish live and breed. Taking a visitor to her lab window atop the Hudson Palisades, Dr. Bell points outside: "It's 400 feet straight down to the river; then there are fifty feet of water, then another 400 feet or more of sediment until you get to bedrock."

The recent history of the river's sediments is of critical importance for plans to dredge toxic chemicals and PCBs out of the river. Man, as "an invasive species," has been stopping some sediments from flowing into the river at dams like Croton in Westchester and Ashokan in the Catskills. These stoppages create sediment catchments around bridges and inside the railroad right of way. "We are trying to find out where the sediment is being transported, to figure out what's new sediment and what's old," says Dr. Bell.

The task is complicated by the Hudson's tides. "During the summer, with the river surface at Albany only four feet higher than it is here, it can take a parcel of water 120 days to get from Albany to the Verrazano bridge — it just sloshes back and forth with the tides. You can see the current's wakes in the river bottom. Sometimes the flood tide creates a sediment wake on the west side of the river, while the ebb tide creates a sediment wake on the east side, so that the river bottom registers water flowing in both directions."

There are other underwater treasures as well. Bell's team has discovered a ten-mile stretch of river bottom that contains some three dozen shipwrecks, including a beautiful 150-foot schooner. They also found four shellfish beds off Nyack which, until the salinity changed some 3,000 years ago, produced oysters the size of dinner plates. They provided 250 calories apiece to the First Americans.

Today's DEC publishes the half-century-old magazine *The Conservationist* and co-publishes the annual *Hudson River Almanac.* The *Almanac's* pages are laden with daily observations taken by thousands of citizens — from grade school kids to "river rats" to professional scientists. Each entry is dated, with proper observation location indicated. Here's a sampler of experiences:

"Snow was three feet deep along the Calamity Brook trail. Signs of wild turkey were imbedded in the crust and the occasional gobble came from back among the beech-balsam understory.

"Redbud, shadbush and dogwood were all in bloom along the river at Edgewater.

"Our first drift of the spring just south of Catskill netted us eighty American shad.

"Using sandworms on the ebbing tide, Carlos Arias caught a forty-five-pound striped bass in the Hudson River at 125th Street and 12th Avenue.

"Herring (alewives) were running up Black Creek from the river. It was as thick a run as we have seen in several years.

"Along my two-and-a-half-mile hike I saw nine bald eagles perched in cottonwoods or out hunting over the river — seven were immature, two were adults."

Observations such as these bear witness to the ever-changing nature of this great waterway. As Fran Dunwell points out: "The story of the Hudson is one of resilience. This is a river whose slogan should be 'Never say die.'"

Bear Mountain: Iona Island on left

Just 12,500 years ago, glaciers of the million-year-long Pleistocene winter receded past Bear Mountain and Iona Island. From this viewpoint on Anthony's Nose, visitors sense the strength of the ice rivers that forcefully carved today's Hudson River channel. Another 4,000 years passed before glaciers withdrew from the Adirondack Mountains *(above)*, the Hudson's northernmost sources. Glaciers that ground through the Adirondacks have left their mark: 1.3 billion-year-old granites remain as bedrock to emerald islands mid-stream in the Upper Hudson. Soils slowly deepened in the post-glacial period. Now there are vast forest stands of pine, fir, cedar, oak, chestnut, hickory and maple, witness to America's earliest statewide conservation programs. Glacial tills deposited throughout the valley provide not only physical memory of the last Ice Age, but also serve as modern day gravel pits.

Coursing waters are a major force in shaping the earth's surface. *(Far left:)* Steady flows of 10,000 years have carved a pool in the granite borders of the Opalescent River.
(Left:) In the mid-Hudson, more recent meanderings have shaped a "Ram's Horn" through the wetlands of Livingston Marsh.
(Over:) As it passes the Catskill Mountains (at right), the Hudson wanders within a broad plain, collecting tributary waters. The river comes to an end 125 miles from here, at the southern tip of Manhattan Island. Subject to four-foot tides twice daily, the estuary portion of the river is often one to two miles wide.

(Left:) Energetic waters from the High Falls of Rondout Creek have cut into 400-million-year-old shales from the Silurian Period of the Paleozoic Era. That's when the Earth's earliest land plants, animals and insects showed up. These wavy, metamorphosed, hard-rock strata served as a significant barrier to lock builders of the 107-mile-long Delaware & Hudson Canal, which followed the Rondout for much of its course. Active from 1826 to 1899, the D&H brought Pennsylvania's anthracite coal to Kingston for river barge delivery via the Hudson.
(Above:) Due to recent milder winters on the nearby Wallkill, Canadian Geese, which only decades ago wintered farther south, now have plenty of water to land on.

Hyde Park: view toward Catskills

(Left:) The popping of spring's leaves spreads a chartreuse carpet from Hyde Park north to the Catskills. Within valley forests a succession of colors announces the developing season. The shad tree's small white blossoms lead off the parade, a sign that the fish of the same name is about to return from its Atlantic feeding grounds to its Hudson spawning grounds. *(Above:)* Native redbud, dogwood and mountain laurel offer a rolling chorus of color into early June. Laurel's pink blush is not its only starring moment. All winter long its evergreen leaves enliven dun-colored forests.

Aquilegia, the elegant botanical name for columbine, is an early spring bloomer at forest edge and meadow boundary. The columbine's five-pointed red crown does a fine job attracting hummingbirds, bees and butterflies to its sweet yellow stamen. Most of the seventy-five different species of columbine in the northern United States can be found in the Hudson Valley. *(Right:)* Not quite as delicate in appearance, the extremely hardy, low-lying prickly pear was an early post-glacial returnee to the valley. It thrives in sandy soils near rocky outcrops. *(Over:)* By early September, arctic fingers creep down from Canada overnight, creating a cold cap over the Hudson's still summery waters. Bird watchers perched here atop Bear Mountain to spot hawks and wildfowl traveling along this major north-south flyway are often treated to misty dawns, and a morning fog that rises to reveal the Hudson Highlands.

(Right:) Light and water play together in the cloud castles we first see as kids and search for again as adults.

(Far right:) Autumn's reflections thrive between wind gusts on the largest of six reservoirs some fifty miles north of New York City. These bodies of fresh water were linked together in the 1800s to form the Croton River Reservoir System.

Croton River Reservoir

Protected within Bear Mountain State Park and the West Point reservation, the Popolopen Creek watershed offers a biological catalog of the post-glacial period. Oak and maple dominate the mixed hardwood forest. Chartreuse in spring, deep green in summer, amber in autumn, white in winter, this view can be seen from a bridge along Route 9W at the point where the Popolopen enters the Hudson near Fort Montgomery.

Iona Island: common reed *(Phragmites australis)*

2: New World to New Nation

This is a very good Land to fall with, and a pleasant Land to see . . . our Master sent John Colman with foure other men in our Boate. . . The Lands they told us were as pleasant with Grasse and Flowers, and goodly trees, as ever they had seene, and very sweet smells came from them.
— from the journal of Robert Juet, first mate on Henry Hudson's *Half Moon* during its voyage up river, Sept. 2–Oct. 4, 1609

Poor John Colman! This member of Henry Hudson's crew, sent to explore what at first glance appeared to be a new Eden, fell to an arrow through his throat launched from two non-welcoming war canoes. Hudson and his men spent the next ten days dealing warily with other native canoe parties as the Europeans probed the areas we now know as Sandy Hook, the Narrows, Staten Island and New York Bay. Englishman Hudson was on his third voyage of exploration for the Dutch East India Company, charged with finding a new route to China. With but eighteen (now seventeen!) men aboard an eighty-ton yacht, he was out to discover, not conquer.

In sight of the island the world would soon call Manhattan, Hudson saw promising signs — a great arm of the sea which had distinct tides, and an incoming tide which would carry his vessel into the land. Might this be the long-sought north passage to the western ocean and the riches of the orient? Before they could find out, Hudson and his men had to keep clear of hostile Indians. Soon enough, they were sailing north at a clip of twenty miles a day. Journal entries record "The Land grew very high and mountainous. The River is full of fish." And finally the natives turned friendly. Juet wrote: "The people of the Countrie came aboard and brought us Grapes, and Pumpkins, which wee bought for trifles."

By October 22, 1609, however, the long boat's crew found the river to "bee at an end for shipping to goe in." Fifty leagues — 150 miles from Manhattan — the hoped-for passage to the Orient lost its tides and its depth, and turned into an ordinary river, climbing up into the Adirondack Mountains. Hudson turned the *Half Moon* down stream and was soon sailing across the Atlantic with news of a rich valley, but no new seaway to the riches of the East Indies.

The Lenape Indian name for the river, Muhheakantuc, translates as "waters in continual motion" or "river that flows two ways." Is it any wonder that reversals of fortune often typify Hudson Valley history?

Within a year of the *Half Moon's* visit, the natives along the Muhheakantuc saw the strange vessels enter their world once more, with Dutch traders anxious to

< **Replica of Henry Hudson's ship *Half Moon***

exchange more "beades, knives and hatchets" for fine beaver pelts. From 1614 to 1617, Fort Nassau, on a mid-river island immediately south of modern day Albany, proved itself to be as good a revenue producer as a Spanish gold mine. By 1621, the Dutch West India Company was chartered in Holland and given the right to establish trading posts and settle the lands in the valley first explored by Henry Hudson aboard the *Half Moon*. A fine fat beaver was set in the middle of the company's great seal. Commissioned as Director General of New Netherland, Peter Minuit led a fleet of colonists west to create a permanent establishment.

Minuit's great bargain — the 1626 purchase of Manhattan Island for goods valued at sixty guilders — provided the Indian sellers with axes, adzes and awls, the cutting edge of technology otherwise unavailable to them. The Lenape chiefs probably did not understand that the Dutch were bargaining for outright ownership of Manhattan Island. Some scholars say that at the time of first contact the Indian sense of land allowed them to grant hunting rights, not ownership. Even for hunting rights alone, the sixty-guilder price was a steal. The letter that carried news of the now-famous purchase back to Holland also catalogued a cargo of furs obtained from the Indians worth some 60,000 guilders.

Modern-day students of anthropology do not view these times as remote. Their ongoing excavations of Dutch and Indian settlements along Esopus and Wallkill creeks, as well as at Ft. Nassau near modern-day Albany, turn up glistening "beades" of glass and copper precisely datable to the period 1609–1624. Careful archaeological analysis of the finds suggests that as time passed, more trade goods were bartered for fewer pelts. By 1640, the Beaver population had gone from plentiful to endangered.

The native populations were endangered as well. Smallpox decimated the Algonkian-speaking Leni-Lenape who had negotiated with Minuit. Dutch aggression also took its toll. A new Director General, Willem Kieft, abhorred the native population. On February 25, 1643, he set in motion a midnight attack at an Indian encampment near Manhattan.

The ensuing conflict, known in history as Kieft's War, saw much of the farmland between the Fort Orange area and Manhattan laid waste — farms burned, families murdered. In February of 1644 the war finally came to an end when Captain John Underhill led a small army of New England mercenaries and Dutch colonists in pitched battles across the area now known as Westchester County. Upwards of five hundred braves were killed, and an uneasy peace was struck.

A diorama at the American Museum of Natural History commemorates the end of that Indian War. Peter Stuyvesant, sent to New Amsterdam to replace the disgraced Kieft, is seen exchanging peace pledges with the Leni-Lenape. The Esopus Indians were accepted as guarantors of the peace by both sides. Over the next hundred years, the dwindling number of Indians who lived below Fort Orange — later Albany — progressively sold off their lands. Town names like Poughkeepsie, Coxsackie, Esopus, Wappinger, Ossining and Mt. Kisco serve as melancholy reminders of olden times.

Families with long histories in the valley are aware that the mode of life of the first settlers of New Netherland and of their immediate descendants was extremely simple. This statement was true not only of the smaller landowners but of many of the patentees of large grants. "From high to low, their lives were the lives of pioneers, lives of hardship, privation and often danger. Roads were few and rough, household belongings modest, and the dwelling that contained more than four rooms was an exception." These words were written in 1928 by a Dutch descendant from Hyde Park in Dutchess County — Franklin Delano Roosevelt, then Governor of the State of New York.

The Dutch Roosevelts had arrived in a place called New Netherland. Not for long. On August 26, 1664, peg-legged Dutch Governor Peter Stuyvesant was alarmed by the sighting of a hostile fleet. Four British men of war, guarding a convoy with 2,000 crack troops, had arrived to claim the colony in the name of its "rightful owner" — the Duke of York. The cosmopolitan merchants of Manhattan (where eighteen languages were spoken by that time) clearly believed that might makes right. The signatures of ninety-three upstanding citizens were rapidly affixed to a document informing their dour governor that they viewed the British commander's assurance that each colonist would be guaranteed "his estate, life and liberty" as generous and agreeable. By September 8, Stuyvesant had signed Articles of Capitulation and was sailing off to Holland with his garrison of 150 troops.

One of the best ways to sense what life was like after the British assumed control is to experience life now along Huguenot Street in New Paltz, Ulster County. The British wanted their new province settled. They were willing to welcome groups of colonists who showed the resources and skills to turn forest into farmland. The quaint university town of New Paltz was founded as a farming community in 1677 by refuge-seeking Huguenots from Palz in the German Palatinate.

After purchasing land from the Esopus Indians, a dozen Huguenot families moved inland from Kingston to establish life on the patent which would be essentially governed by twelve of their own elders — the Duisin or Dozen — for a century. The documents of their purchase, still part of the New Paltz town records, show the Esopus Indians receiving kettles, axes, adzes, shirts, white and black net-work, stockings, lead, powder, knives, wine, oars, duffel, blankets, needles, awls, tobacco, and two horses. The Hugenots received clear title, registered as a patent by the English, to 40,000 acres.

Huguenot families have lived in Ulster County for over three centuries. Huguenot Street in New Paltz is more than the nation's oldest continually occupied (and beautifully restored) street. It is also home of the Dutch Reformed Church (the French speakers eventually became Dutch and later English speakers), where the community gathers and welcomes visitors each Sunday. You are also welcome at their monthly community dinners. It is highly likely that you will be seated with a descendant of one of the Dozen, perfectly willing to recount their history of persecution for the "sin" of reading Scripture at home without a priest. Sunday night bible study in private homes is still a New Paltz tradition.

Religion, however, ranks far below commerce as a reason for settlement along the Hudson. In the first half of the eighteenth century, Albany's traders thrived on furs brought to market by the Iroquois, and the produce of expanding farms in the upper Hudson, Mohawk and Champlain valleys. New York merchants built up their own fleet of ocean-going cargo vessels and traded New York's produce with the Far East and Europe. Pirates like Captain William Kidd were welcomed home in the port of New York. Once the merchants of Manhattan found a way to wealth, they never forgot it.

In between Manhattan and Albany, the colonial economy of the Hudson Valley revolved around large manor estates. If you want a three-dimensional experience of life and work in those days, you can time-transport yourself back to the 1700s by visiting Philipsburg Manor, Upper Mills, in the village of Sleepy Hollow. As you walk across the oaken dam that spans the Pocantico River you hear the grist-mill's waterwheel plop-plopping, you see Historic Hudson Valley's colonially-clad interpreters working with the barn animals, a bonneted woman carrying garden produce into the manor house kitchen. Soon enough your tour group enters the Philipse family's prime possession, the flour mill, where every three months the millstones would get so smooth that the master miller, an enslaved African named Caesar, would have to take the mill apart to re-dress or roughen up the millstone surfaces.

The Philipse family had twenty-two slaves working at their Upper Mills. Yet most of those who lived on the Philipse's 92,000 acres 250 years ago were tenant farmers. As your guide the miller puts it: "The arrangement with Mr. Philipse was a simple one. You and your family came into New York City with no money in your pocket. He would meet you at his city office and say 'Look — I have a good deal for you. Come up and live on my property in the Hudson River Valley. Do anything you want — put up a house, barn, fences, have animals, raise children — but you have to grow wheat and pay me ten percent of all you grow.

"That seems like a good deal. Except that only Mr. Philipse has a mill, and he takes ten percent of your flour as his milling fee. And the manor house is also the manor store . . . and Mr. Philipse sets the price for the wheat he buys from you and the products you buy from him. He has the land, his mill uses the flowing water, his stones use the power of gravity, his tenants do the work."

Philipse Manor covered the whole lower part of Westchester County, from Tarrytown to Yonkers. The Philipse ships carried wheat to the Caribbean where they loaded sugar to take to England. The ship's return cargo to New York was trade goods and more prospective tenants. Other big manors farther up river included Van Cortlandt Manor, Beekman Manor, and Livingston Manor.

By 1750 the Hudson Valley was well settled with farming communities. The colonial frontier with the Indians was now to the north and west. Beyond lay French Canada and their legions of loyal Indian warriors, a threat to further British expansion on the continent. In the summer of 1754, the prosperous trading community of Albany welcomed a Congress of delegates from Pennsylvania, Maryland and the New England provinces. Their goal: to assure the Iroquois Nation's loyalty in the event of war with France.

The alliance proved a vital factor in the Seven Years' War which soon broke out. This conflict, during which the Mohawk Valley and upper Hudson were avenues of continual warfare, gained Canada and much of the Caribbean for the British, but virtually bankrupted the British treasury. The Stamp Act and several other measures passed by Parliament in London provoked cries of taxation without representation and forged unity and a spirit of independence in English-speaking North America.

Weapons of Colonial New York. *(Far left:)* The Van Rensselaer Cannon, cast in 1630 at an Amsterdam bronze foundry and bearing the monogram of the Dutch West India company. New York State Museum. *(Upper left:)* A London-made big bore matchlock commonly used on remote farmsteads in the late seventeenth century. *(Lower left:)* British flintlock musket of 1760 owned by the City of New York and turned over to the Continental Congress in 1775 for issue to the First New York Regiment. West Point Museum Collection, USMA.

By the autumn of 1774, when the First Continental Congress was meeting in Philadelphia, productivity in the Hudson Valley had made New York the third largest port in the British Empire, preceded only by London and Philadelphia. In the spring of 1775, the shots heard around the world were fired at Lexington and Concord, Massachusetts. On July 3, General George Washington took command of the Continental Army on Cambridge Common. On March 17, 1776, the artillery captured from the British at Ticonderoga and Crown Point, New York was mounted on the heights overlooking Boston and the British were soon forced to evacuate. George Washington headed south to defend New York City.

Control of the river that flows two ways would be a determining factor in the Revolution's outcome. New York's Provincial Congress had already cautioned the Continental Congress that British mastery of the Hudson would "divide our strength and enfeeble every effort for our common preservation and security." The Philadelphia delegates agreed, but the lower Hudson's broad expanses offered no adequate defensive positions. The best opportunity for that was provided by a sixteen-mile stretch through the Hudson Highlands above Peekskill.

In August of 1776, New York's Harbor once again hosted a British invasion fleet — not four men of war, but twenty-four; not 2,000 soldiers as in 1664, but 32,000, augmented by 13,000 seaman. George Washington and his continental and provincial novices found themselves facing fully forty percent of Great Britain's warring capacity — the largest expeditionary force of the eighteenth century.

Fighting and retreating, fighting and regrouping, disappearing into the forests and the fog, learning with every mistake — and there were scores of them — the Americans were pushed back in 1776 at the Battle of Long Island, the Battle of Harlem Heights, the Battle of White Plains. They surrendered nearly 3,000 at poorly conceived Fort Washington, situated in today's Washington Heights on Manhattan Island.

Fortifications up river also proved insufficient a year later. Tory betrayal of approach routes to river-covering Forts Montgomery and Clinton at the southern approach to the Highlands led to a late-afternoon battle and American defeat in October 1777. A minor fort on Constitution Island, opposite West Point, was quickly taken as well.

The Redcoat force of 2,500 under Sir Henry Clinton got back in their boats and sailed north on the river he called "the Key of America." They burned the state capital at Kingston, destroyed patriot Robert Livingston's home at Clermont and expected to join forces with General John Burgoyne's army heading down from Canada. Unexpectedly, Clinton received news of Burgoyne's defeat farther up the Hudson. Now it was time for the British to weep.

The British attempt to invade from Canada by descending through the Lake Champlain corridor had not gone smoothly. Patriot generals Horatio Gates and Benedict Arnold, leading 20,000 Continentals and militia, had captured 5,000 British regulars at the pivotal battle of Saratoga. The tides of war had turned. A surge of Bluecoats was headed Clinton's way. Sir Henry sailed south to New York City. Washington now controlled the Hudson from the Highlands north.

General Washington's command, issued in late 1777, was clear: "Seize the present opportunity and employ your whole force and all the means in your power for erecting and completing . . . such works and obstructions as may be necessary to defend and secure the river." The eventual result was Fortress West Point, which spans the Hudson Highlands. The American flag has flown there since January 27, 1778, making it the oldest continuously-manned post of the U.S. Army.

European expertise helped the Americans to capitalize on the "present opportunity." British guns captured at Saratoga were soon manned by American artillerymen at West Point. The French, impressed by the Saratoga victory, cast their lot with the Americans against a common enemy, the British. Shiploads of troops and arms came to Washington's support. The engineering competency of Polish General Thaddeus Kosciuszko energized the patriots' picks and shovels to build a multi-fort ring of fire around the Point.

Meanwhile, the Americans set about blocking the Hudson's waters as well. A giant wooden boom spanned the Hudson River between Constitution Island and West Point. The barrier was designed to slow British warships intent on ramming its upstream neighbor, a log-floated 500-foot long chain. Its 120-pound links had been forged by local blacksmiths at the Sterling Ironworks — ahead of schedule and under budget!

The Plain at West Point is certainly the U.S. Army's most hallowed training terrain. In July of 1779, light infantry were arduously drilled here by the Continental Line's imported taskmaster, Friedrich von Steuben, after Washington and his aides spied on approaching British forces from a nearby mountain. These crack troops followed General "Mad Anthony" Wayne in a midnight bayonet raid on nearby Stony Point (now a State Park Historic Site). The cost to the British: one recently-taken fort at the mouth of the Hudson Highlands, 600 regulars, and a good store of fine weapons. The cost to the Americans: fifteen casualties.

So much for the idea of another easy British campaign up river! They never challenged West Point by force again, but they did attempt to take it by treachery in 1780. Though appointed West Point's commander, General Benedict Arnold was dissatisfied with his treatment by the Continental Congress. Saratoga's hero sought to better his lot by switching sides. Twenty thousand pounds sterling was Arnold's price for intentionally degrading West Point's defenses and delivering the plans of West Point to the British Adjutant Major John André. André's capture as a spy nipped the budding plot. Arnold fled downstream to British-held New York City. His name now appears in history books as a synonym for traitor. Washington immediately took over command and mobilized the militia.

Successfully protected by the Highlands fortifications, the Continental Line prepared for a final showdown. A quick march into the South in 1781 put surprise on the American side. In alliance with French troops commanded by General Rochambeau and the French Caribbean Fleet under Admiral de Grasse, Washington besieged Yorktown, Virginia. Once Lord Cornwallis capitulated with his army of 7,000, the War for Independence was won. Washington and his army returned to their safe haven in the Hudson Valley and waited two years for a peace treaty.

Washington's Headquarters was at Hasbrouck House in Newburgh, the first historic site ever to be preserved by the American people. Eight thousand troops of the Continental Army were encamped at nearby New Windsor. With their pay in arrears, their pleas for pensions turned aside, the soldiers viewed the Congress of their new Republic with great disdain. Some entertained radical remedies — monarchy or mutiny. To a Colonel's lightly veiled suggestion that the best remedy for a weak republic was an American monarchy with George I on the throne, Washington replied, "I must view with abhorrence and reprehend with severity" any such schemes.

On March 15, 1783, a dissident group within Washington's Army made a move to mutiny. They were convinced that only a change in commanding generals would see their demands for pay and benefits satisfied by the Continental Congress. Washington arrived uninvited at the mutineers' meeting. While his cool, rational exposition of the proper course to seek their back pay failed to fully sway them, the revelation of his fragility did the trick. Reaching into his jacket for a pair of reading spectacles he had never before worn in public, he explained, "Gentlemen, you must pardon me. I have grown gray in your service and now find myself growing blind." The depth of his personal commitment so struck the officers at this moment that the eyes of many filled with tears and the mutiny was abandoned.

Having defended the Hudson against invaders and the new republic against mutineers, Washington rode into New York City in triumph on November 25, 1783. As the King's troops, accompanied by a large body of Loyalists, prepared to set sail for England, Washington prepared to return to the life of a Virginia planter. He would be home at Mt. Vernon by Christmas Eve.

Among the Loyalists who left New York to find a home in exile in England was Frederick Philipse III of Philipsburg Manor. He left with what he presumed was absolute title to his manor, but as he lay dying in 1785, arrangements for public auction of his seized lands were underway. Some 300 individuals would pay a pittance for farms which 270 tenant families had rented from the manor lord. History in the Hudson Valley, in harmony with its river, always flows two ways.

On September 16, 1609, Robert Juet, Henry Hudson's first mate, entered in his journal: "This morning the people came aboord, and brought us eares of Indian Corne, and Pumpkins, and Tobacco: which we bought for trifles." Exploring the river's west bank, Hudson's crew found "good ground for Corne and other Garden herbs."

Other entries in Juet's log noted "Our Boat went to fish, and caught great store of very good fish." During their four weeks Hudson's crew feasted on "Mullets, Breames, Bases and Barbils." The Hudson still serves as spawning ground to all of the fish the First American and early Dutch settlers depended on for food.

The Pocantico River in Sleepy Hollow, north of Tarrytown, powered Frederick Philipse's grain mill, which served as Philipsburg Manor's industrial center. Born in Holland in 1626, Philipse came to New Netherlands during Peter Stuyvesant's governorship. He rapidly augmented his earnings as Stuyvesant's carpenter by chartering vessels to trade with other American colonies. He used profits from his ventures to buy more land from the Indians. Philipse readily joined other Dutch colonists as they switched allegiance to the conquering English in 1664. By 1674, ten years after the Union Jack was raised, he was not only an alderman but also the wealthiest man in New York City. By the 1680s he owned one third of Westchester County.

A strong supporter of the Dutch Reformed Church, Philipse honored *Sinterklaas* in the Christmas Season by setting out three oranges, evoking the Saint's dower for three poor girls. Dutch was used as a language of worship in the Hudson Valley until the early 1800s.

Tenant farmers on Philipsburg Manor strove for self-sufficiency. Wool from their sheep provided them with yarn for their weaving. Flax, a cultivated field crop, provided linen for the family's summer cloth needs. Natural dyes were drawn from the surrounding forests. Today's visitors to the spring weekend "sheep to shawl" event will find the twenty-acre colonial farm brimming with demonstrations of colonial crafts. During the summer months, local schoolchildren can attend week-long day camps here. Their hands-on tasks in barn, field and farmhouse make valley history far more immediate than a textbook.

The slaves' garden at Philipsburg Manor faithfully presents the plantings of 1750: sweet and white potatoes, kidney and black-eyed beans, cayenne pepper, pumpkin or winter squash, greens and medicinal herbs, plus vegetables raised to be sold to European settlers. Modern research has determined that in 1750, twenty-two of the twenty-four people living at Philipsburg Manor in Sleepy Hollow were slaves. New Yorkers owned 21,000 slaves in 1790, making it the second largest slave holding state of the newly free nation. *(Bottom right:)* Some twenty miles south in Yonkers, Philipse Manor Hall, now a New York State Parks Historic Site, was the country seat of manor lord Frederick Philipse III until the outbreak of the American Revolution. With the American triumph Philipse lost all of his holdings.

Philipsburg Manor

Yonkers: Philipse Manor Hall

Van Cortlandt Manor's first rooms were built by Stephanus Van Cortlandt in 1680. In the early 1700s, the family owned 86,000 acres from the Croton River to Peekskill. Tenant families worked farms averaging 225 acres. Land rent equaled twenty bushels of wheat. The Van Cortlandts lived here for seven generations, or 250 years. This Historic Hudson Valley house museum is filled with colonial period pieces, many once owned by the family. Though aristocratic landlords who delighted in gracious grounds and gardens, the Van Cortlandts were patriots. By the time the American Revolution broke out, Pierre Van Cortlandt, the Manor Lord, became New York State's first lieutenant governor. Pierre's son Phillip was colonel of the Fourth New York Regiment and led his troops in many Revolutionary War battles.

The Van Cortlandts greeted their visitors with Chinese tea served in Chinese porcelain and sweetmeats preserved in sugar and served in English porcelain. Today's summer visitors to Van Cortlandt Manor can make reservations for colonial dinners and entertainments. They are offered in a great tent near the Ferry House Inn, where the Van Cortlandts once hosted travelers on the Albany Post Road.

Colonial cooking demonstrations and open hearth cooking courses at Philipsburg Manor feature Native American, African, Dutch and English recipes. Prized souvenir: bags of stone ground corn and wheat from the Pocantico River-powered gristmill.

Peekskill: replica of British frigate, *HMS Rose*

(Far left:) The British established their power in 1664 with regiments of regulars and ships of the line.
(Left:) They also "established" the Church of England but showed tolerance to all other faiths. Now flanked by the twin towers of the World Trade Center, St. Paul's Chapel has welcomed worshipers since 1763. After the Revolution, St. Paul's became part of America's newly-formed Episcopal Church.

"Pinkster," the lively Dutch Pentecost that comes fifty days after Easter, celebrates the descent of the Holy Spirit. New York's slaves — and they were one in eight people living in colonial New York — joined their masters in the festivities. Modern Pinkster Weekend at Philipsburg Manor gives Historic Hudson Valley an opportunity to spotlight both the important tasks fulfilled by Africans during New York's early days (such as yarn making), as well as African cultural traditions preserved or developed after the slaves' passage to the New World.

Both British and Americans believed control of the Hudson Valley was vital to success in the Revolutionary War. In the summer of 1776 the brothers Howe, General and Admiral, arrived in New York Harbor with forty percent of the Crown's war-fighting ability. Peekskill lay at the dividing line between the area around New York, held by the British from 1776 until 1783, and the Hudson Highlands stronghold of George Washington. The British broke the first chain across the Hudson at Fort Montgomery in October of 1777 and burned the State Capital at Kingston before news of Burgoyne's defeat at Saratoga sent them back down river. Today the Brigade of the American Revolution re-enacts the encampments (*right*) and the burning of Kingston (*far right*).

America's hero on the Saratoga battlefield was bold troop leader Benedict Arnold. When General John Burgoyne's campaign from Canada ended in defeat in the upper Hudson Valley, George III's cause lost an army of 5,000, George Washington got an artillery train for his new Fortress West Point, and the French decided to support the American Revolution. By 1780 a disgruntled Arnold turned traitor by scheming to betray his command at West Point.

Benedict Arnold

Saratoga marker honoring Arnold

While spying against British forces campaigning around New York City in September of 1776, Nathan Hale was caught and hanged without benefit of trial as a traitor to the Crown. The statue of Hale, bound at the ankles, reminds all Americans of the words the patriot offered on his Manhattan gallows: "I only regret that I have but one life to lose for my country."

Dawn at Fort Putnam highlights but one of fourteen forts and redoubts that made up the fortress at the "west point" of the Hudson River. Sailing vessels had to virtually stop while negotiating this s-curve, fifty miles north of New York City. A chain-and-log boom was placed across the curve in 1778. With thousands of militia awaiting call by beacon fires along the Hudson, and 8,000 Continental Line troops encamped at nearby New Windsor, Washington made his headquarters at Newburgh with confidence. He was never besieged. The Badge of Merit Washington first awarded here in 1782 is the nation's oldest decoration—the Purple Heart.

New Windsor: First Purple Heart

Newburgh: Hasbrouck House, Washington's headquarters

After the Treaty of Paris was signed on September 3, 1783, the British speeded up withdrawal from their Thirteen Colonies. When General Washington entered New York on December 4, 1783, the American Revolution came to an end. The Hudson was again a river of free passage. Six years later, on April 30, 1789, Robert Livingston of Clermont, Livingston Manor, now Chancellor of New York's Supreme Court, administered the Presidential Oath of Office to George Washington. As the First President of the United States kissed the offered bible, Livingston was heard to say, "tis done." Washington's inaugural address pledged "that the foundations of our national policy will be laid in the pure and immutable principles of private morality." Dioramas, documents and displays at the site of the National Park Service's Federal Hall Museum illuminate that first year of constitutional government, when New York served as the nation's capital.

In October of 1777, the British who burned Kingston sailed up-river and put to the torch the homes of Margaret Beekman Livingston and her son, Robert Livingston, Jr. Undaunted, the Livingstons rebuilt, and their holdings survived the Revolution. As Continental Congress Delegate, Livingston served on the committee that drafted the Declaration of Independence. As Ambassador to France he helped make the Louisiana Purchase; as investor he sponsored Fulton's steamboat, the *Clermont*.

3: Country Seat to the Empire State

A little, old-fashioned stone mansion, all made up of gable ends, and as full of angles and corners as an old cocked hat.
— Washington Irving's description of his home in Tarrytown, New York

Washington Irving, America's first successful author, propelled the Hudson Valley into the nation's consciousness with his eerie legends and tongue-in-cheek "history" of New Netherlands. Irving's fictional characters, like the headless horseman of "The Legend of Sleepy Hollow" and the twenty-year Catskill napper Rip Van Winkle, had brought him international acclaim and financial success. New Yorkers of every flavor were delighted to discover in his *History of New-York* a mythical Dutch heritage that included, among others, the Van Brummels (the first inventors of Mush and Milk), the Van Klotens of Kaatskill (Horrible quaffers of New Cider), the Van Pelts (mighty hunters of Minks and Muskrats), and the Van Nests of Kinderhook (Valiant Robbers of Bird's Nests). Until this time, New Yorkers had been so preoccupied with the bustle of trade and commerce that they had hardly considered "culture."

Irving's most fanciful nom-de-plume was Diedrich Knickerbocker. This mythological author came to New York's attention on November, 1809 through a series of literary notices in the *Evening Post* explaining his mysterious disappearance and asking for information about his whereabouts. In the process these news items announced the impending publication, in its two volumes, of *A History of New-York,* "published in order to discharge certain debts [Knickerbocker] has left behind." This literary hoax initiated a New York tradition — book promotion.

Irving's creations have made their way into our national folkways in other ways as well. The name "Knickerbocker" has become a standard nickname for a New Yorker (hence basketball's New York Knicks). Irving's coinage of "Gotham" as a nickname for the city is still in use. His celebration of the ancient English yuletide celebrations at Bracebridge Hall not only helped reinvent Christmas in America, but sparked its revival in England as well. His script about the encounter between a headless specter and New England schoolmaster Ichabod Crane continues to inspire Halloween "hauntings." Most importantly, Irving's revival of Dutch folklore and the Dutch-style restoration of his home at Sunnyside established a valley-wide ethic for preserving and conserving "pleasant associations and quaint characteristics."

The neighborhood of Irving's Sunnyside was north of New York City on the river's eastern shore. Today's visitors will encounter several history-filled river towns

before they reach the Hudson Highlands. They are Yonkers, Hastings-on-Hudson, Dobbs Ferry, Irvington, Tarrytown, Sleepy Hollow, Briarcliff Manor, Ossining, Croton-on-Hudson, Cortlandt and Peekskill. Their nineteenth-century growth from local agricultural markets into thriving manufacturing centers and rural residences of city workers was tied to the development of the steam engine.

The steam-powered transportation revolution was the engine of economic development within the valley. Until 1807 travelers usually headed north by Hudson River sloop — a three-day voyage to Albany, depending on winds and tide. If you went by land, horses could take you thirty miles a day on the old Albany Post Road. (That 160-mile route, world famous as Broadway, is still followed by today's Route 9).

On August 17, 1807, the steamboat chugged into Hudson Valley history. Robert Fulton had invented the first practical paddle wheeler and named it *The North River Packet of Clermont* to honor the home estate of his partner and principal investor, Robert R. Livingston, Jr. ("The Chancellor"), co-drafter of the Declaration of Independence. The Livingston clan's two manors had prospered with the end of the American Revolution. In 1806, well before Fulton had completed his invention, Livingston had arranged to have the New York legislature grant him a monopoly on Hudson steamboat traffic.

With the Clermont making three round trips to Albany each week, another nickname soon emerged: Livingston Valley. By 1811, the Fulton-designed and Pittsburgh-built *New Orleans* was steaming along the Mississippi. And Chancellor Livingston's cousin, Harriet, had become Mrs. Robert Fulton.

Steamboat traffic along the Hudson boomed by 1825. The Fulton-Livingston monopoly had just been overturned in the courts and fourteen competing paddle wheelers were churning their way up and down the river. On October 25 a cannon salvo fired at Buffalo was relayed battery by battery through the Mohawk Valley and then down the Hudson — 550 miles of explosive celebration heralding the departure of the first barges to travel through Governor DeWitt Clinton's 363-mile-long, 82-lock Erie Canal. On their arrival in New York, Governor Clinton emptied a cask of Lake Erie water into the tidal waters at Manhattan's Battery. America's heartland, opened up by the world's longest canal, was now linked to that world through America's Valley. American ingenuity and engineering had jumped over the geologic obstacles that had halted Henry Hudson. For the next century, the port of New York controlled fully half of the nation's international commerce.

Steam locomotives were soon chugging along the shoreline. The Hudson River Railroad reached Peekskill by 1849, Albany by 1851. The ice-clogged river, closed to

The Steamer **MARY POWELL.** Capt. Ferdinand Frost.

navigation for three winter months, was no longer an impediment to commerce and personal movement within the Valley.

Back from the shore, the nineteenth century saw rapid economic development in the river towns. The same steam engines at work on the river and railroad were changing industry from large handcraft shops into standardized parts factories. Demand for labor brought a flow of Irish and Germans into the valley. They enlarged the Erie Canal and built the canal linking the upper Hudson through Lake Champlain to Canada. They built the Croton Dam and its supporting aqueduct system in Westchester to slake New York City's thirst. Immigrants worked Mr. Otis's elevator factory in Yonkers, the brass tube mills in Dobbs Ferry, or the Rockland County riverside gravel pits that filled city-bound barges. Produce, milk and leather goods found markets down river. The arrival of the railroads allowed locals to commute to new jobs in the city. Real estate developers built rows of houses and invited the expanding middle class to a better life in the suburbs.

Each of the town's main streets pointed at the railroad station: Once boarded, passengers were (and still are) treated to one of America's most beautiful rolling panoramas. Heading south from Peekskill are first the two-mile-wide expanses of

THE SCENERY OF THE HUDSON.
VIEW. NEAR "ANTHONYS NOSE"

Haverstraw Bay and the Tappan Zee, set before the Ramapo Mountains; then come the towering basaltic pillars of the Palisades.

Today's tourists in the lower Hudson's historic river towns can view architectural history by searching out the treasure trove of Victorian era windows embellishing both business and residential buildings. Modern architecture treats windows as something to look out from. Victorians viewed windows as something to look *at*. These inner town streets of yesterday's America were designed for strolling "eyes up." They are decorated with an endless variation of arches and columns, marbles and bricks. Masons drew on Hudson Valley quarries for marble, riverside gravel pits and cement plants for their raw materials. Nineteenth-century builders delighted in festooning their Neo-Gothic structures with faceted masonry, jigsawed brackets and undulating borders — eye candy. It's easy to know where the interesting old architecture is: just go to the train station and stroll within a mile radius. Victorians did not park their horses in the town lot; they walked to their Hudson Railroad trains. And the elegant churches they worshipped in, many of which host magnificent sets of Tiffany windows, are topped by enough different kinds of spires to constitute a virtual pattern book for church architects.

Each Hudson River town offers its own variation on the theme of economic progress. The town now known as Beacon on the eastern shore of the river, sixty miles north of New York City, tapped the power of a Fishkill Creek waterfall to run the Matteawan Company's cloth mill complex. In 1832 hundreds were employed in the cluster of brick buildings that today houses offices, artist's live-in lofts and a streamside restaurant. Beacon's business life was not unlike other valley towns: market town for local farmers who were feeding an ever-expanding New York City, mill town for a growing nation whose commerce was creating new millionaires daily. Everything could be shipped by boat or rail from the Hudson River waterfront, either down-valley to New York and overseas, or inland to an ever-expanding national economy. Also, the valley served as brickyard, cement source, and gravel pit for New York City's masons.

In their *Art of the Landscape,* Kathleen Johnson and Tim Steinhoff, writing for the non-profit Historic Hudson Valley, offer insights into artistic explorations that began within the Hudson Valley during the age of Washington Irving:

"The area witnessed an explosion of cultural expression, the first internationally recognized American artistic and literary statement. Spurred on by the valley's scenic beauty, artists, writers, architects and gardeners offered up a new Eden . . . and helped shape [the young nation's] character."

The stars of the visual branch of the Hudson River School were the painters Thomas Cole, Asher Durand, Alfred Bierstadt and Frederick Church. Their canvases conveyed a romantic view of nature, celebrated the national spirit of exploration, and inspired appreciation of the beauty of the American Landscape. The poet William Cullen Bryant waxed rhapsodic about the religious experience a visit to the American wilderness offered.

Inspired by such visions of nature, Andrew Jackson Downing, America's first professional landscape gardener, virtually invented American landscape design along the banks of the Hudson. In 1847 Downing, writing in *The Horticulturist,* extolled "the landscape-gardening beauties that are developing themselves every day, with the advancing prosperity of the country." Speaking of the stretch of old Livingston descendants' estates which in the late twentieth century would be protected within our largest National Landmark Historic District, he wrote, "For twenty miles here, on the eastern shore, the banks are nearly a continuous succession of fine seats. . . Surrounded by extensive pleasure grounds, fine woods or parks, even the adjoining estates are often concealed from that part of the grounds around the house. . . One might fancy himself a thousand miles from all crowded and busy haunts of men."

Downing and his disciples Calvert Vaux and Frederick Law Olmstead devised their "genteel romantic landscapes" in the valley. Then, in 1867 Vaux and Olmstead went down valley to carve and preen 900 shambly acres into Central Park, viewed by Manhattan Island residents as their "pleasure grounds."

By 1867, the Hudson River Railroad was owned by entrepreneur Cornelius Vanderbilt, himself born at the mouth of the Hudson on Staten Island. Starting out with his own pole- and sail-powered cargo boat at the age of sixteen, Vanderbilt had carried produce across the harbor to New York City. In his twenties he was captaining swift steamboats that defied the Livingston monopoly by stealthily running from Manhattan to New Brunswick, New Jersey. Soon enough he owned sternwheelers, then ocean-going steamers connecting New York City to San Francisco and Le Havre in France. The small fortune he had made on the water was invested on shore, where he cunningly amassed a greater fortune. Vanderbilt cornered the stock of a flock of separate railroad companies by clever trading on the New York Stock Exchange, consolidated them into the New York Central and pushed straight through to Chicago in 1873. America's vital artery into its heartland coursed at sea level through the Hudson Valley, then made a 500-foot climb by railroad or canal locks to Lake Erie, Chicago and beyond.

Vanderbilt was perhaps the most prominent of the newly wealthy who were soon marrying into "old" valley families and adding their own magnificent country seats to the estates already lining the river. By century's end architects such as Alexander Jackson Davis and Stanford White would provide clients such as the Vanderbilts, the Millses and the Mortons with Classic Revival, Neo-Gothic and Beaux Arts beauties. Those who had recently amassed their fortunes often spent lavishly and conspicuously, while the older families — whether out of "breeding" or lack of means — were usually more conservative and retiring. Cornelius Vanderbilt's grandson, Frederick, ensconced in his Stanford White-designed palace at Hyde Park, hardly minded the steely clatter of the family's railroad at water's edge.

The novels of Edith Wharton can endow a "great estate" visitor's eyes with a vision of how the high life was dutifully enjoyed in the decades around the turn of the century. She was born into the New York social life of which she wrote. True New York socialites were frequently summer guests at the Cliff Walk mansions of Newport, Rhode Island, invitees to the racing events at Saratoga, and to the spring and fall seasons in the Hudson Valley. And, most importantly, to the winter social season in New York, when The Four Hundred confirmed who they were upon receipt of Mrs. Astor's invitation to dance in her Fifth Avenue mansion's ballroom, which could comfortably accommodate only 400 guests. Wharton lived in and visited many a Hudson Valley mansion. Here is a brief description of the "arcaded hall" in Mills Mansion (the fictional "Bellomont" in her novel *The House of Mirth):* "On the crimson carpet a deerhound and two or three spaniels dozed luxuriously before the fire, and the light from the great central lantern overhead shed a brightness on the women's hair and struck sparks from their jewels as they moved."

Those who were not members of this elite would take excursions up river at a brisk twenty knots, looking left and right at the country seats of the newly rich and famous. They could only look, because they were not open to the general public.

Even if brief or vicarious, a visit along the river was always memorable. Karl Baedeker, whose name is interchangeable with "guidebook," wrote that the Hudson was more beautiful than his fatherland's Rhine. Hudson Valley-based naturalist John Burroughs echoed Baedeker's sentiment: "In summer, a passage up or down its course in one of the day steamers is as near an idyll of travel as can be had, anywhere in the world."

Sunnyside: entry to "Little Mediterranean" pond

Sunnyside: grounds designed by Irving for his walks

Two centuries of Livingstons lived at Montgomery Place. Walking through its rooms, one still gets a sense of continuous occupancy from encounters with the family's elegant French antiques and their practical American electrical gadgets. The estate's romantic gardens, forest paths by falling waters, and beautiful picnicking grounds have been restored to their mid-nineteenth century horticultural splendor. Andrew Jackson Davis's nursery at Newburgh provided many of the original plantings. Modern visitors who pick and pay for berries and fruits from the estate's extensive orchards get a sweet taste of Hudson Valley agricultural life.

Montgomery Place: Alexander Jackson Davis's neo-classical facade

Montgomery place: Andrew Jackson Downing-inspired gardens

From cottage to castle, the Hudson Valley's "genteel romantics" set the pace for nineteenth century American domestic architecture. With a splendid choice of Gothic-influenced country homes being constructed up river, the work of architect Alexander Jackson Davis was often featured in New York-based national publications. Estate grounds were given as much consideration as the buildings they surrounded. Visitors would approach a country seat through a grand *allée* of trees. Andrew Jackson Downing, pioneering horticulturist and landscape designer from Newburgh, provided many of his clients with a variety of flowering specimens, such as the star magnolia, to herald spring's arrival. The Dean's House is a perfect fulfillment of the Neo-Gothic Hudson Valley Bracketed style developed by Davis. West Point was one of the nation's first planned communities, satisfying the housing needs of the US Military Academy's officer instructors.

When the television show *America's Castles* showed viewers through the labyrinthine Mohonk Mountain House in New Paltz, they were following the trail of more than 3,000,000 visitors. Founded in 1872 by Quaker twins, Alfred and Albert Smiley, Mohonk provides for its sojourners now as they did then—on the American Plan. Five hundred guests warm themselves by 150 wood-burning fireplaces, enjoy murder mystery weekends in the winter, mountain climbing lessons in the summer. The Mohonk Mountain House of today is a 2,200-acre National Historic Landmark, surrounded by the member-supported 6,400-acre Mohonk Preserve.

New York City's expanding need for water provided a rationale for much-needed forest conservation in the lower Hudson. The Croton River network of reservoirs, begun in the 1840s, enlarged in the late nineteenth century, created a six-reservoir Westchester and Putnam County greenbelt. The Croton Dam was heralded as the eighth wonder of the world, ranking just behind the Great Pyramid of Egypt in masonry bulk. In the twentieth century, a six-reservoir Catskills system was established. Side benefits: the Old Croton Aqueduct right of way is now a favorite jogging path, and the city's reservoir system, stocked with bass and trout, has a great fishing program.

Manhattan's Hudson River shoreline for the seven miles stretching north from 72nd St. has long been a lovely collection of green havens. Frederick Law Olmstead, the designer of Central Park, completed his grand plan for Riverside Drive and its adjoining Riverside Park in 1909. Two important Riverside Park landmarks are Grant's Tomb at 122nd St., commemorating the Civil War, and the Soldiers and Sailors' Monument at 89th St., commemorating the Spanish-American War.

Riverside Park: Soldiers and Sailors' Monument

Manhattan: the Cloisters, Fort Tryon Park

Catskill was an important port for Robert Fulton's *Clermont* as the Hudson became a steamboat lane in 1807. Passengers landing on Catskill Creek proceeded west by stagecoach and wagon. Barges and freight steamers took livestock, farm produce, bricks and blue stone to city markets. In 1884 forty icehouses shipped 1,000,000 tons to New York City. Today's New Yorkers come upstream in their pleasure craft, stopping at Catskill Creek's marina after a day of nautical exploration. Recently Cedar Grove, home of the Hudson River School's founding painter Thomas Cole, underwent restoration. The Greene County Historical Society, Cedar Grove's owner, wants to welcome visitors into Cole's studio, where he instructed his student Frederic Church. Church's home, Olana,

is just across the river in Columbia County.

Columbia County's historic farmsteads, including those immediately surrounding Frederic Church's fabled Olana, are part of a coherent landscape that has merited broad preservationist efforts. The concept of "viewshed" protection is a Hudson Valley innovation. Land trusts and conservancies, working with organizations such as Scenic Hudson, Hudson River Heritage, Friends of the Hudson Valley and New York State's Hudson River Valley Greenway, have acquired land and conservation easements, and purchased development rights from farmers. In this way they help preserve the rural character and agricultural economic activity that assures the valley's overall health.

Christmas Callers in the mid-Hudson have many festively-decorated house museums to visit. Mills Mansion is one of the stars on the circuit, with its Stanford White-designed dining room, its twenty-four-foot-tall Christmas tree with German decorations, and its gallery of Clermont Livingstons—Robert the Judge, his wife Margaret Beekman Livingston, and their son, Robert the Chancellor.

Staatsburg: dining room at Mills Mansion

Mills Mansion: Livingston relatives of Mills family

In the Pocantico Hills of Westchester, Dutch settlers gave a 400-foot summit the name Kykuit, which means lookout or high point. Searching for a country home site near his brother William's riverfront estate, Rockwood Hall, John D. Rockefeller and his eighteen-year-old son JDR Jr. climbed to the top of this hill. In 1892 father and son set about accumulating, parcel by parcel, a 3,000-acre estate. The Classical Revival Rockefeller mansion, was initiated in 1907 and expanded to its present size by 1913. Three hundred acres surrounding Kykuit were fenced off to assure family privacy. For years the public has had access to miles of Rockefeller bridle and hiking trails, while four generations of Rockefellers made Kykuit their home. The mansion itself opened up to the public in 1994. It is now owned by the National Trust for Historic Preservation and maintained by the Rockefeller Brothers Fund. Guided tours of Kykuit leave from Historic Hudson Valley's Philipsburg Manor Visitor's Center.

The Kykuit tour includes the formal Rose Garden, Nelson Rockefeller's modern sculpture collection (his painting galleries are seen on the house tour), and Hudson views from elegantly planted terraces.
(Far right:) The Oceanus fountain emulates the 1576 centerpiece of Florence's Boboli Gardens. Nearly 1,000 acres of the original estate, as well as Rockwood Hall's riverfront mile, are now part of Rockefeller State Park.

4: America's Valley

Few estates like [those from the turn of the century] survived the imposition
of the income tax, progressive inheritance taxes and the Depression . . .
The Hyde Park of the Vanderbilts was enjoyed by only one generation.
— The Great Estates Region of the Hudson Valley

If Washington Irving's hero Rip Van Winkle had happened to sleep through World War I and its aftermath instead of the War of American Independence, he might have been as astonished at the disappearance of servant-supported opulence as he was by the disappearance of the British monarchy from the colonial Hudson Valley. While the culture of the turn of the century had emphasized wealth, privilege, and display, that of the twentieth heralded the age of the common man.

With the advent of mass-produced automobiles, the un-bejeweled masses expanded their invasion of the Hudson Valley, the Catskills and the Adirondacks in search of vacation havens. Now they arrived not only as passengers on steamers and railroads but at the wheel of their own Fords. Resort hotels of every ethnic flavor and boarding houses offered heat-fleeing city families a "two weeks in the cool country" seat. The Bear Mountain Bridge opened in 1924, providing vacationing automobilists their first cross-Hudson roadway. In the Roaring '20s bootleggers made regular runs to the Catskill resort hotels along Burgoyne's invasion route, carrying bottles of freshly distilled "Canadian Club." Borscht Belt comedians forged a self-deprecating brand of humor quickly popularized on the vaudeville stage. In the audience were the Irish, German, Italian and Jewish families who had provided brain and brawn to create the valley's built environment, its industry and commerce.

As the century progressed, river ferries gave way to a network of cross-river bridges. The George Washington Bridge and New York State Bridge Authority's Mid-Hudson and Rip Van Winkle spans were built before World War II. New York City's construction czar, Robert Moses, poured concrete north — the Henry Hudson, Sawmill and Taconic Parkways were also underway by the 1930s. Destinations to be reached via these parkways were meant to be recreational, not commercial — no trucks were allowed.

The growth of business was slowed down enormously by the worldwide economic depression of the 1930s. After World War II, International Business Machines, which had developed its punched paper time card system and electrical tabulators in Endicott, New York, expanded into electronic computers at Poughkeepsie. When childless Frederick Vanderbilt's niece could find no buyers for her late uncle's estate in 1938, nearby Hyde Park neighbor President Franklin D. Roosevelt saw to it that one of the first acquisitions of the Historic Monuments Division of the National Park Service was Vanderbilt Mansion.

Roosevelt created a new style of national leadership: born into privilege, he reached out to those born without it. The Roosevelt vision has also left a strong impact on today's valley. By 1941, while he was still President, visitors to Hyde Park could enjoy the FDR-designed Dutch Colonial style library he had built on his property. This pioneering Presidential Library and Museum houses his Presidential papers and memorabilia as well as much of his personal stamp and antiquarian collections. Scholars and nostalgia lovers find a good chunk of both our national and Hudson Valley heritage there. After the president's death in 1945, the Roosevelt family home, Springwood, also came under the care of the National Park Service.

FDR's influence on local architecture did not stop at the borders of his estate. The post offices of Rhinebeck, Beacon, Wappinger Falls, Poughkeepsie and Hyde Park were all built during the Depression in a Dutch Colonial design researched and approved by the President. All were decorated with local history murals. Those at the Rhinebeck post office, narrating historical valley incidents from Henry Hudson's 1609 visit to the 1939 post office dedication, were created by Olin Dows, a local artist with Livingston blood lines.

In the 1980s Val-Kill, Eleanor Roosevelt's private country retreat since 1924, became the third Roosevelt site in the town of Hyde Park. Few today would contest a guide book claim that she was the most influential and admired woman in American history. As the first pro-active First Lady, she inspired social reforms not only within the White House but across the nation. In her city townhouse and at Springwood, she had been "under the thumb of her imperious mother-in-law, Sara Delano Roosevelt," as a *New York Times* writer has noted. Val-Kill became her refuge. This was home base for Ambassador Roosevelt when she pushed the Declaration of Human Rights through the United Nations and traveled across the world as our ambassador-at-large. Curtis Roosevelt chose his words fondly as he observed "My grandmother's warmth and concern for others can still be felt in her cottage's cluttered simplicity."

Eleanor Roosevelt's voice can be heard today on a tape available at the Roosevelt Site bookstore. Her welcome is warm, her shared insights give personal dimension to objects. Recalling the 1939 overnight Hyde Park visit of the King and Queen of England, her wit is pungent: "My husband said 'they will be tired, they will want a cocktail.' My mother-in-law firmly said, 'I'm quite sure the King would prefer a nice hot cup of tea.' When they came in my husband said to the King, 'I have cocktails, but my mother thinks that you would rather have a hot cup of tea.' The King looked at him and said 'My mother would have said the same thing, but I will have a cocktail.'

Who hasn't heard the comedian's one liner "New York's a great place to visit but I wouldn't want to live there?" Let's amend that to "New York's a great place to live, so long as you live it up along the Hudson." People who live in the mid-Hudson know that down river there's a lively big town. Manhattan is headquarters for hundreds of American and multinational companies. City dwellers and visitors, in need of respite from surging information and bustling crowds, travel up river to experience tranquility. America's Valley offers naturally dramatic landscapes, elegant mansions, Victorian Main Streets as respite from Gotham's turbulence. Folks from the mid-Hudson, seeking respite from tranquility, often include the world's most capital city on the valley tour they give visitors.

The Dutch West India Company merchants settled a great river valley to exploit its economic potential. Yet much of the Northeast has seen the South and West participate more fully in the economic expansion at the end of the twentieth century. Jobs have flown away. Business-oriented organizations like Mid-Hudson Patterns for Progress and Team Hudson focus their efforts on bringing quality jobs into the Hudson River Valley, so that children educated in the valley can stay here. One major asset they are helping to develop is Stewart Airport at Newburgh. Initiated as West Point's flight training facility, it was recently given up by the military and privatized. It has some of the longest runways in the world, and is the site of a new world trade center and expanding regional distribution facilities. "There is a balance we need to honor," says Gerry Davidson, Executive Director of the Ulster County Development Corporation, "using the river to help us live, but at the same time preserving it so that it's worth living here."

Being a tourist in the Hudson Valley is not like visiting Orlando, Florida, where professionally-staffed entertainment parks and talking animatronic figures do all the work for you. The notable sights are spread out around the valley, and sometimes you may have to put some sweat equity into searching them out. "Heritage tourism" — a combination of visits to historic sites, guided or self-guided tours, background reading and the visitor's own powers of imagination — is currently enjoying a boom here. Turn left or right and you will find a window into the 1600s, the 1700s, the 1800s and the 1900s. Or slip into a whitewater kayak and live in the *now!*

The Hudson is a great place to visit, and it's an even better place to volunteer. Many valley newcomers and "second homers" don't enjoy feeling like outsiders. They learn quickly that the way to gain acceptance from the locals is to help staff the fundraising shad bakes, music festivals, and harvest fairs that cram each valley weekend's schedule of events. Visitors quickly note that locals have volunteered money as well as time to support a host of organizations that have made the region a pioneer in the self-rescue movement.

Three valley organizations that have spearheaded environmental and land conservation movements along the Hudson and inspired scores of similar organizations all across the country are Sloop Clearwater, Scenic Hudson and Riverkeeper.

Clearwater is known for mid-river environmental education programs aboard their 110-foot replica Hudson River sloop. A summer-long schedule of fundraising festivals, featuring folksingers or freshly-picked corn or strawberry shortcake keeps towns up and down the river aware of the Hudson's needs. Scenic Hudson has pioneered legal means of assuring that coherent natural landscapes are preserved, that valuable townscapes are restored and enjoyed. Their Storm King Mountain lawsuit established

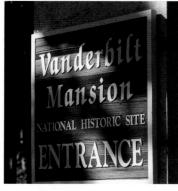

Ossining's Victorian Crescent. The nearby Visitor Center with a Sing Sing cell and an electric chair provide a taste of hard-life history.

a national legal precedent allowing organizations to sue on behalf of our natural heritage. Riverkeeper is a volunteer-sponsored environmental watchdog which, working with Pace University's Environmental Litigation Clinic, has won more than a hundred federal cases against polluters.

No finer habitat for the human soul exists than Scenic Hudson's 120-acre park called Poets' Walk. You will find it 100 miles north of Manhattan. On Poets' Walk you pay attention to details. Wildflowers, purple and blue, standing together amidst grass which will soon go to seed. White dandelion heads waiting for a wind; clusters of clover; day-end light glinting off May's dogwoods. Couples who have left their cars behind walk through the landscape, like figures in an old engraving. Across the path, a wild turkey struts, then runs, then lofts into its nighttime roost. Benches backed with curving cedar boughs are placed at viewpoints where the path descends, a meadow opens, a view beckons the eye. Here is a chance to sit and slowly scan points near and far.

After a rest, you walk up a gentle rise to a grand gazebo. By its side is a long-handled pump and water from within the earth. You look out from the knoll-top shelter and there is the river glowing. Sports fishermen in small boats — the striped bass are running. Overhead — warbling, chittering and precise, screechy whistles: a springtime date, perhaps a mate, a nest and next year's spring song?

The sun is moving to its hiding spot behind the Catskills — but is it the sun that's moving? At Poets' Walk, you sense that the land is turning away from the sun, the river's tidal waters are being pulled by the moon. When the sun returns the earth will have revolved, and another day's walk in the valley will await you.

Salisbury Mills: steam train excursion on Moodna Viaduct

The lives of President Franklin Delano and First Lady Eleanor Roosevelt are the focus of the Presidential Library and Museum of the National Archives adjacent to Springwood in Hyde Park. The museum explores FDR's rise to prominence and the turbulent mid years of "The American Century." Eleanor's nearby cottage, Val-Kill, honors her integrity as First Lady and her campaign for Human Rights at the UN. The homes and gardens at Val-Kill and Springwood, FDR's birthplace, are watched over by the National Park Service.

There are thirty-one significant public gardens on both sides of the sea-level portion of the valley. *(Preceding page:)* Wave Hill was once home to author Mark Twain and orchestral conductor Arturo Toscanini. It is now a 28-acre oasis supported by members and located in the Riverdale section of the Bronx. *(Above:)* Spring's arrival in Ft. Tryon's Crescent Park starts a three-week surge of blooms that ripples up the river. The tulips loved in April near the George Washington Bridge open in time for Albany's mid-May Tulip Festival. Many families that fled Nazi Germany came to this Washington Heights neighborhood and brought their kids here to play. Memories formed in Ft. Tryon Park are now honored by park benches and garden plots endowed in the name of departed parents.

Not all blooms are within gardens. Orchards offer salvos of apple and cherry and peach and pear blossoms. The valley is virtually in bloom throughout April and May. More and more farmers are offering organically-grown fruits, berries and produce for sale at their own farm stands or at green markets. Apple varieties picked in early autumn are MacIntosh, Cortlandts, Pippins, Empires and Golden Delicious. Apple cider has been a favorite refreshment since Rip Van Winkle's time. *(Over:)* Pow-wows gather Native Americans living in the New York metropolitan area. Sterling Forest's Renaissance Faire in Tuxedo draws 150,000 to merriment on August and September weekends.

Old Rhinebeck Aerodrome's weekend air shows take space-age visitors back to Flying Circus times. Visionary airplane restorer Cole Palen's Rhinebeck museum exhibits fabric-covered planes named SPAD XIII, AVRO 504K, Curtiss Jenny, Sopworth Snipe. The stage offers a glamorous glimpse of lady's fashions in the days of the Red Baron and Captain Eddie Rickenbacker. Thrilling reenactments of WW I Dogfights are launched from the airstrip.

Mills Mansion's "Gathering of Old Cars" welcomes roadsters with rumble seats, "woodies" and a burnished "T." These cars don't speed through town; if they did the folks at the wheel couldn't respond to all the friendly waves that greet their stately procession.

(Preceding page:) Marist College's crew practices on waters made famous by the Poughkeepsie Regatta. From 1895 to 1949, the National Championships were decided here. Marist is known for integrating computer technology, developed in the valley, into the teaching and learning process. Dennis Murray, Marist's president, has this to say about the valley's colleges: "There are a lot of great institutions in this country, but I think the very best places are set in an environment that helps inspire the students."*(Above:)* Founded in 1861, Vassar was one of the first women's colleges. Its graduates were leaders of the suffragette movement that gave women their voting rights in 1920. Is it any wonder that the first American institution to offer courses in drama had among its graduates Jane Fonda and Meryl Streep? In 1969, as the First Man landed on the moon, the first male arrived on Vassar's campus. A graduation week

tradition soon faced possible extinction: How would the new co-eds look bearing the fabled Vassar Daisy Chain? In an effective compromise, males were enlisted as "ushers" to escort the females carrying the floral cordon. In 1976, as America celebrated its Bicentennial, the first female cadets joined The Corps at the United States Military Academy. West Point is America's oldest engineering college. Its engineers mapped the expanding nation, designed canals and their intricate locks, tamed flood-prone waterways, and erected coastal fortifications. Touring West Point and its museum, you learn that fifty-five of the sixty major battles of the Civil War had West Point commanders on both sides. Twentieth-century American military leaders Pershing, MacArthur, Patton, Eisenhower and Schwarzkopf all paraded from The Plain into history.

Memorial Day ceremonies on the Carrier *Intrepid's* flight deck salute all who gave their last full measure of devotion. During World War II her flight deck launched planes into combat over the Marshall Islands, Truk, Leyte Gulf, and Okinawa. *Intrepid* participated in astronaut recovery, the Cuban Missile Crisis surveillance, and the Vietnamese War. *(Right:)* Fourth of July fireworks at Clermont Historic Site, 100 miles north, recall the difficult summer of 1776 when Robert R. Livingston, Jr., a member of the Committee that drafted the Declaration of Independence, was scurrying around Long Island and Manhattan Island, secretly marshalling resistance to the invading British troops.

From October to March, Bear Mountain's rink welcomes 120,000 skaters. Summer visitors — five million — come for the hiking, camping, swimming on three forest-rimmed lakes, rowing on Hessian Lake, and feasting at Bear Mountain Inn.

Most sailors on the Hudson's frozen surface belong to the Hudson River Ice Yacht Club. They patiently wait for arctic temperatures and winds so they can speed along Tivoli South Bay at

speeds above seventy miles an hour. Many of these wood-beamed boats were crafted at the end of the nineteenth century. Their original owners could beat the train from Rhinebeck to Poughkeepsie. The youthful Franklin Roosevelt used to speed along the frozen Hudson in his *Hawk*. Another Roosevelt family racer, the *Icicle*, is now permanently displayed at the Hudson River Maritime Museum in Kingston.

Biologist Chris Letts with planked shad

The Hudson is once more providing fishermen with wide smiles rather than tall tales of "what used to be." Striped Bass Derbies and Shad Bakes are waterfront rites of spring that benefit rod and gun clubs up and down the river. *(Far right:)* Fly fishermen prefer their solitude along a stream that is still home to native rainbow trout.

Membership in the Hudson River Boat & Yacht Club Association is 10,000 strong, with thirty-six boat clubs based in thirty towns. Sailors are underway every weekend in regattas sponsored by the Haverstraw Bay and Hudson River Yacht Racing Associations.
(Right:) Improving water quality has encouraged lifeguard-attended public bathing beaches, such as this one at Croton Point Park.

(Far left:) Summer adventurers ride waters that will eventually arrive in New York City's water system. *(Left:)* The vertical faces of the Shawangunk range offer the best technical mountain climbing challenges in the Northeast. The fabled "Gunks" lie within member-supported Mohonk Preserve.

A Guide to Treasures of the Hudson River Valley

Letters in parentheses refer to location letters at top of map

CULTURAL SITES

American Museum of
  Fire Fighting (L)
117 Harry Howard Avenue
Hudson, NY 12534
518-828-7695

Bardavon 1869 Opera House (H)
35 Market Street
Poughkeepsie, NY 12601
845-473-5288
www.bardavon.org

Bear Mountain Inn (F)
Bear Mountain State Park
Route 9W
Bear Mountain, NY 10911
845-786-2701

Caramoor Center for
  Music and Arts (E)
149 Girdle Ridge Road
PO Box 816
Katonah, NY 10536
914-232-5035
www.caramoor.com

The Center for Performing
  Arts at Rhinebeck (J)
PO Box 148
Rhinebeck, NY 12572
845-876-3080

Clearwater-
Hudson River Sloop (H)
112 Little Market Street
Poughkeepsie, NY 12601
845-454-7673
www.clearwater.org

Culinary Institute of America (I)
Route 9
Hyde Park, NY 12538
845-452-9600

Foundry Museum (F)
Putnam County
  Historical Association
63 Chestnut Street
Cold Spring, NY 10516
845-265-4010

Franklin D Roosevelt Library
  and Museum (I)
511 Albany Post Road
Hyde Park, NY 12538
845-229-8114
www.nps.gov/hofr

Harness Racing Museum
  & Hall of Fame (F)
240 Main Street PO Box 590
Goshen, NY 10924
845-294-6330

Edward Hopper House and
  Hopper House Art Center
82 North Broadway
Nyack, NY 10960
845-358-0774

Hudson River Maritime Museum (J)
1 Rondout Landing
Kingston, NY 12401
845-338-0071

Hudson River Museum
  of Westchester (C)
511 Warburton Avenue
Yonkers, NY 10701
914-963-4550

Hudson Valley
  Children's Museum (D)
21C Burd Street
Nyack, NY 10960
845-358-2191

Intrepid Sea Air Space Museum (B)
Pier 86
West 46th Street at 12th Avenue
New York, NY 10036
212-245-0072
www.intrepid-museum.com

Museum of the Hudson
  Highlands (G)
The Boulevard PO Box 181
Cornwall-on-Hudson, NY 12520
845-534-7781

Museum Village (F)
1010 Route 17M
Monroe, NY 10950
845-782-8247

National Museum of Dance (R)
99 South Broadway
Saratoga Springs, NY 12866
518-584-2225

Neuberger Museum of Art (D)
State University of New York
  at Purchase
735 Anderson Hill Road
Purchase, NY 10577
914-251-6100

New York State Museum (O)
Empire State Plaza
Madison Avenue
Albany, NY 12230
518-474-5877

The Old Rhinebeck Aerodrome (J)
Stone Church Road PO Box 229
Rhinebeck, NY 12572
845-758-8610
www.oldrhinebeck.org

Opus 40 and
  Quarryman's Museum (K)
7480 Fite Road
Saugerties, NY 12477
845-246-3400

Paramount Center for the Arts (E)
1008 Brown Street
Peekskill, NY 10566
845-739-2333

Saratoga Performing Arts Center (R)
19 Roosevelt Drive
Saratoga Springs, NY 12866
518-587-3330
www.spac.org

Shaker Museum and Library (N)
88 Shaker Museum Road
Old Chatham, NY 12136
518-794-9100
www.shakermuseumoldchat.org

South Street Seaport (B)
South and Fulton Street
New York, NY 10038
212-732-8257
www.southstreetseaport.com

Storm King Art Center (F)
Old Pleasant Hill Road
  PO Box 280
Mountainville, NY 10953
845-534-3115

Vassar College (H)
Frances Loeb Lehman Art Center
124 Raymond Avenue PO Box 23
Poughkeepsie, NY 12604
845-437-7000
www.vassun.vassar.edu

HISTORIC SITES

Boscobel (F)
Boscobel Restoration, Inc.
1601 Route 9D
Garrison-on-Hudson, NY 10524
845-265-3638
www.boscobel.org

Cherry Hill (O)
523 1/2 South Pearl Street
Albany, NY 12202
518-434-4791

Clermont (K)
State Historic Site
One Clermont Avenue
Germantown, NY 12526
518-537-4240
www.friendsofclermont.org

Clinton House (H)
State Historic Site
PO Box 88 549 Main Street
Poughkeepsie, NY 12602
845-471-1630

The Cloisters (C)
The Metropolitan Museum of Art
Fort Tryon Park
New York, NY 10040
212-923-3700
www.metmuseum.org

Crailo (O)
State Historic Site
9 1/2 Riverside Avenue
Rensselaer, NY 12144
518-463-8738

*Continued on page facing
other side of map*

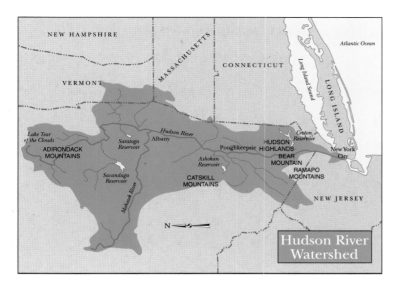

Hudson River Watershed

HUDSON RIVER CRUISES

Circle Line Cruises
Pier 83 West 42nd Street
at 12th Avenue
New York, NY 10036
212-563-3200
www.circleline.com

Dutch Apple Cruises
PO Box 395
Albany, NY 12202
518-463-0220

Hudson Highlands Cruises
"Commander"
PO Box 355
Cornwall-on-Hudson, NY 12520
845-534-7245

Hudson River Adventures
"Pride of the Hudson"
100 Brower Road
Monroe, NY 10950
845-782-0685

Hudson River Cruises
"Rip Van Winkle"
PO Box 333
Rifton, NY 12471
800-843-7472

New York Waterway
12th Avenue at 38th Street
New York, NY 10018
800-533-3779

TOURISM OFFICES

Adirondack North Country
Association
Adirondack, NY 12808
518-494-2515

Albany County Convention
& Visitors Bureau
1-800-258-3582
www.albany.org

Columbia County Tourism
1-800-724-1846
www.columbiacountyny.com

Dutchess County Tourism
Promotion Agency
3 Neptune Road
Poughkeepsie, NY 12601
1-800-455-3131
www.dutchesstourism.com

Greene County Tourism
Box 527, TG99
Catskill, NY 12414
1-800-355-CATS Ext. 86
www.greene-ny.com

Historic Hudson Valley
150 White Plains Road
Tarrytown, NY 10591
914-631-8200
www.hudsonvalley.org

Hudson River Heritage
Rte 9 PO Box 287
Rhinebeck, NY 12572
845-876-2474
hudsonriverheritage.org

Hudson River Valley Greenway
Capitol Building, Room 254
Albany, NY 12224
518-473-3835
www.hudsongreenway.state.ny.us

Hudson Valley Tourism
1-800-232-4782
www.hudsonriver.com

Hudson Valley Tourism
Development Council
308 Clinton Avenue
Kingston, NY 12401
845-339-8399

National Trust For Historic
Preservation
www.nthp.org

New York State Bridge Authority
Mid-Hudson Bridge Plaza
Poughkeepsie, NY 12602
845-691-7245

NYC and Company
Convention & Visitors Services Inc.
810 7th Avenue
New York, NY 10019
212-484-1222
www.nycvisit.com

New York State
Department of Commerce
Division of Tourism
1 Commerce Plaza
Albany, NY 12245
1-800-CALL-NYS
www.iloveny.state.ny.us

New York State Department of
Environmental Conservation
New Paltz, NY 12561
845-255-5453
www.dec.state.ny.us

New York State Office of Parks,
Recreation and Historic
Preservation
Albany, NY 12238
518-474-0456
www.nysparks.com

New York State Office of Parks,
Recreation and Historic
Preservation - Taconic Region
Staatsburg, NY 12580
845-889-4100

Orange County Tourism
Suite 111, 30 Matthews St
Goshen, NY 10924
845-291-2136
www.orangetourism.org

Palisades Interstate Park Commission
Bear Mountain State Park
Bear Mountain, NY 10911
845-786-2701
www.nysparks.com

Putnam County Tourism
1-800-470-4854
www.visitputnam.org

Rensselaer County Tourism
1-800-732-8259
www.nyslgti.gen.ny.us/Rensselaer/

Rockland County Tourism
3 Main Street
Nyack, NY 10960
800-295-5723
www.rockland.org

Scenic Hudson
9 Vassar St.
Poughkeepsie, NY 12601
845-473-4440
www.scenichudson.org

Troy's RiverSpark Visitor Center
251 River Street
Troy, NY 12180
518-270-8667

Ulster County Tourism
PO Box 1800
Kingston, NY 12402
1-800-DIAL-UCO
www.co.ulster.ny.us

Visitors Information Center
United States Military Academy
West Point, NY 10996
845-938-2638
www.usma.edu/guide-page

Westchester Convention
& Visitors Bureau, Ltd.
235 Mamaroneck Avenue
White Plains, NY 10605
1-800-833-9282
www.westchesterny.com

Additional Hudson Valley Web Sites:
hvnet.com
www.pojonews.com
www.enjoyhv.com

(Right:) Hiking trails and bikeways within Manhattan's Riverside Park and Henry Hudson Parkway cross into the Palisades Interstate Park via the George Washington Bridge. The Palisades' trails lead fifty miles north to Bear Mountain. The Hudson River Valley Greenway has opened and linked 300 miles for hiking and biking.

(Far right:) Golfers can play at dozens of public courses, such as the Garrison Country Club. More than one hundred golf courses, public and private, lie between Manhattan and Albany.

Hands-on experiences at county fairs bring kids in contact with animals like those that their great-grandparents tended. SummerWeek History Day Camps and "Sheep-to-Shawl" events at Philipsburg Manor and elsewhere help suburban kids understand traditional farm chores. Local farm youth are interested in modern agricultural production and marketing developments. Ulster County alone, with 70,000 acres of farmland, has twenty-eight 4H Youth Development Clubs supporting 400 members. County fairs valley-wide feature 4H crop and animal projects.

Philipsburg Manor: herding sheep

Philipsburg Manor: shearing a sheep

Percherons

Driving "Six-in-Hand," competitors put teams through the paces at the Dutchess County Fair. Percherons, harnessed for show, braided for beauty, will soon enter the ring to "walk, trot, and drive-on," tracing intricate patterns in perfect harmony. English, Western, Driving, and Pulling events fill the Fair's six days.

Dutchess County dairymen

The antique farm implements on display here demonstrate changes in farming techniques. *(At left:)* Farming activity has also changed. During this Grand Champion's life, the dairy farming community of Dutchess County has shrunk from 275 to thirty-seven. During the same period, farm stands selling fresh produce direct to the public at retail prices have grown from ten to over 120. Rhinebeck's fairgrounds, busy most weekends from May into October, welcomes tens of thousands during New York's second largest agricultural fair.

(Left:) Since 1863, this beautiful course has made Saratoga Springs "the summer place to be." With six weeks of thoroughbred racing from the nation's leading stables, a multi-million dollar thoroughbred yearling sale, a social season punctuated by elegant fundraising benefits at the National Museum of Racing, owners speed around as much as their horses.
(Above:) Orange County's Goshen is home to the Harness Racing Museum and Hall of Fame.

Sculpture in outdoor spaces has three spectacular homes: Albany's Empire State Plaza in front of the State Capitol, the Storm King Art Center in Orange County, and the Kendall Sculpture Gardens at Pepsico's Headquarters in Purchase. Their world class collections are set in elegantly-designed landscapes; Empire State Plaza sits atop an amazing gallery of abstract expressionist paintings.

Storm King Art Center: Alexander Lieberman's *Iliad* ∧

ᵥ **Purchase: George Segal's *Three Friends on Four Benches***

Saratoga Performing Arts Center offers a great Jazz weekend around Independence Day, The New York City Ballet in July, the Philadelphia Orchestra during August, and a host of every-thing-else-in-between. *(Right:)* Free West Point Band Summer Sunday Concerts at Trophy Point continue musical traditions begun in 1778.

(Right:) The final leg of Sloop *Clearwater's* October Pumpkin Cruise takes it past the New Jersey and New York Palisades. For thirty years, this fundraiser has brought thousands to riverfront environmental awareness exhibits. *(Far right:)* Fall harvest time brings apples, grapes and pumpkins. The vinifera grapes are gathered and pressed, starting their way into European style wineries along the Dutchess and Shawangunk Wine Trails.

Croton Point Park: Hudson Harvest Fair

Agri-tourism puts discerning consumers in direct contact with farmers. The Hudson Valley Harvest Program publishes locally available county Farm Produce Maps. Dutchess County Tourism, working with Cornell University's Cooperative Extension Program, furthers the concept "Buy Local…Ensure Future Harvests" through "u-pick-em" promotions.

Antiquers prowl the streets of towns like Nyack, Cold Spring, Hudson and Saratoga Springs, where dozens of shops offer thousands of heirlooms past and future. Antique fairs, flea markets, and estate sales are the sites of intensive search-and-buy weekends. Antiques-oriented articles and publications, appraisal fundraisers, and a heightened interest in all things collectible have fueled the recent antiques boom.

Manhattan: Sloop *Providence* approaching George Washington Bridge

A flotilla of historic-replica sailing vessels now carries America's maritime heritage and environmental goals forward. Sloop *Clearwater,* founded by folk singer Pete Seeger and friends in 1969, led the way. The Clearwater organization is now 12,000 members strong. The 110-foot-long sloop's seventeen-person crew includes six members who volunteer for one-week cruises.

Manhattan: UN General Assembly building and Secretariat

With 189 flags waving at United Nations Headquarters, 140 languages spoken in its neighborhoods, and trade links across the modern world, Manhattan sometimes pays little attention to its neighboring river. It should. America's Valley offers a valuable window into time.

Manhattan: WNBC staffers at annual caroling